Preface:

Dear Reader,

Today's World is getting completely transformed because of the advent of the digital age. To survive and thrive in this digital age, one needs to upgrade oneself in the digital space. This is highly recommended for a successful social and professional life.

I have developed the Workbook *"Transform – Personal to Digital"* based on my experiences in the Digital world from last 10 years. This Workbook will give you a first-hand experience of the Digital World based on a set of exercises that you will be carrying out yourself.

Once you complete the exercises mentioned in this Workbook, you would be ready to launch or relaunch successfully your Social and Professional life in the Digital space in a dynamic manner.

As this is a Workbook which I have completed myself, I would be available to guide the readers through the exercises mentioned in this Workbook.

You can reach me at sanjaynair005@gmail.com for any queries or guidance required for completing this Workbook.

With Best Wishes and Regards,

Sanjay Nair

About the Author:

Sanjay Nair is a Professional Consultant with more than 16 years of Experience in the field of Marketing and Commercialization. After working with reputed companies Nationally and Internationally, Sanjay Nair now runs his own Consulting firm in Hyderabad, India.

You can reach Sanjay Nair at his email id: sanjaynair005@gmail.com

Contents:

Transform - Personal to Digital: I don't want to be left alone

Introduction:

Transformation is something which is consistent with this age. With the advent of unbelievable connectivity through Digital world, everyone inadvertently needs to transform themselves consistently so that they are not left behind in this highly competitive environment. *"Transform – Personal to Digital"* is a workbook which will help you to create a digital footprint as per your desire and needs. This will be done through a series of exercises which will hasten the self-learning process in your journey from Personal to Digital.

I. **My Personal World is Creepy:**

Today's reality is that everybody around us whether we like or not are online in some or the other way. They maybe our family members or our friends or colleagues from our work place or total strangers whom we meet every day because of varied circumstances. In this kind of scenario, our personal world starts looking little creepy and fearsome if we have not consistently updated ourselves in multiple respects.

The bellow mentioned exercise would give you the creepiness index around your personal world.

Exercise 1: Ask 5 people around you and find out what they are doing in the top 15 Social Networking Sites and make notes on the same

1. Facebook
2. YouTube
3. Instagram
4. Twitter
5. Reddit
6. Pinterest
7. Vine
8. Ask.fm
9. Tumblr
10. Flickr
11. Google+
12. LinkedIn
13. VK
14. ClassMates
15. Meetup

II. I am not growing:

In today's environment it is not uncommon to feel that you are struck in some way and everything around "you" is moving very fast. There is a profound sense of feeling that you are struck, and you are not growing. This is the bane of the digital world which makes you feel unworthy instantly if you are not connected to the larger digital network out there. There is no choice today. You must be digitally connected in every possible sense.

The bellow mentioned exercise will take you an inch forward to the digital world.

Exercise 2: Start with Facebook as an experiment and then move forward.

1. Join Groups of Interest
2. Keep the Image Consistent – Select a good personal Image and keep it Consistent for some time.
3. Be Active and interact with Friends and Group Members
4. Create Content of various Interests. Be versatile on creating Content.
5. Study people who are influencing the discourse and follow them to understand the trends they are setting.
6. Fall back on the area of your expertise and share as much as you can.
7. Keep Interacting and ask Questions
8. Discussions are a sure way to engage yourself in Groups
9. Fallback and look how you are progressing

III. The Fear of the Digital World:

Initially the digital world looks like a giant octopus out there to devour you and your persona. Whatever you do looks like meaningless when, so much is happening around you. Yes, it's a predatory world but the fear of this predatory world can be overcome by starting small and expanding at a consistent pace. Your digital world or network can start with the people you already know and thereafter you can slowly expand to likeminded people and groups in the digital world. This way your confidence increases on a daily basis.

The bellow mentioned exercise will help you to overcome the fear of the digital world and online Social Media.

Exercise 3: Carry out the bellow exercise to overcome the fear of Social Media

1. Keep the selfies to a minimum

2. Post in the Evening, Night, or Midnight
3. Less hashtags and it's better
4. Don't try to be Funny if you are not
5. Filters to be Utilized in Moderation
6. Detailed explanations are not needed for everything you do – Post regularly but maybe once in a day.
7. If you are going places, then tag yourself with Locations to create interest in your friend circle and groups
8. Go to the Memory lane – Use Black and White Images to create special impact
9. Give Likes and Take Likes – Engage

IV.   The First step forward:

The first step is the hardest but the most essential. It is the defining moment when you give a personality to your Digital self. The first step creates the foundation on which you build your digital life in a gradual manner.

The bellow mentioned exercise will help you to take your first step forward in the digital world.

Exercise 4: Research, Retrace and Recreate your Personality in the Digital World by carrying out the bellow mentioned exercise

1. Research yourself online
2. Look into the past – Analyze your Digital reputation
3. Be on your guard – Use Presence of Mind as you work on your Digital personality
4. Don't Overexpose yourself – Privacy is important too
5. Any Chinks in the Armor? – Fix what is that is Fixable
6. Publicize the productive Content
7. Keep going forward with the Good work

V.   Your Professional and Social profile:

It is very important to segregate your professional and social profile in the digital world. Your Professional profile will give you, your bread and butter. In other words, your professional profile is the source for your income and livelihood.

On the other hand, your social profile is for giving you that sense of support that you expect from your friends and family or for connecting with new people and groups for sharing likeminded hobbies and interests. Unless you are a star of your own reckoning, it's better to keep your professional and social profiles separate.

The bellow mentioned exercise will help you to create your own professional and social profile.

Exercise 5: Create a Professional and Social profile based on the bellow guidelines

Guidelines for Online Professional Profile:

1. "About Me" – This is the most important part. Describe in few words but give a high punch
2. Link Forward
3. Link Backward
4. Add some Spice
5. Work Experience should be the most logical and measurable
6. Study and Education part – Create a Nostalgic effect
7. Be open with the kind of work you are seeking
8. Circulate your Profile in every possible way
9. Select an Image consistent with your profile
10. Leap forward with your Personal Brand building

Guidelines for a Successful Social Media Profile:

1. Your Name – Has to be your Real Name
2. Your Username – Should Reflect your Personal Branding thoughts
3. Your Profile Pic – Should be Consistent
4. Your Link – Other Sites, Other Pages
5. Your Bio – Make it Spicy and Hot
6. Your Interests – Don't skip this part
7. Your Background – Part of Personal Brand Building
8. Your Privacy Settings – Keep many things under wrap. Don't over expose
9. Your Activity – Engage with Groups and Friends with Good Content
10. Your Promotion – Obviously Good Work needs to be highlighted

VI. How to meet people from your Digital World:

The aim of joining the digital world should be eventually to meet more and more people and thus increase your professional and social network. The more you meet people from your professional network, the more you have scope to enhance your earnings and income. The more you meet people from your social life, the more exciting and colorful your personal life becomes.

The bellow mentioned exercise will help you to meet people from your Digital World.

Exercise 6: Find Out Events and Activities that are taking place in the Online Groups and Communities that you have joined and then plan for effective Networking by actually attending them.

1. Explore Different Venues and Groups – And Attend the Events
2. Prepare the Questions based on your needs – And ask them
3. Interact with the Key players – Take Information and Give Information
4. Follow-up on Your Conversations – With More information or further Questions
5. Stay in touch – Create a long-term relationship

VII. Great Digital Stories - Case Studies

People have made big with their digital life. New stars are born daily who have hit the jackpot through the digital route. The bellow are some case studies of big time successful digital stories.

Exercise 7: Study the bellow mentioned 28 most successful personal digital stories and analyze how the digital platform has helped these people achieve superstardom.

1. Kanye West
2. Joy Cho
3. James Corden
4. Laci Green
5. Josh Holz and Daniel Lara
6. DJ Khaled
7. Johnetta Elzie and DeRayMckesson
8. J.K. Rowling
9. Felix Arvid Ulf Kjellberg (a.k.a. PewDiePie)
10. Donald Trump
11. Lele Pons
12. Cristiano Ronaldo.
13. Caitlyn Jenner.
14. Essena O'Neill
15. Narendra Modi
16. Elise Andrew
17. Ken M
18. Lilly Singh (a.k.a. Superwoman)
19. Matt Drudge
20. Angie Nwandu

21. Andrew Bachelor (a.k.a. King Bach)
22. Kayla Itsines
23. Peter Bouckaert
24. Kim Kardashian West
25. Josh Ostrovsky (a.k.a. The Fat Jew)
26. Drake
27. Tess Holliday
28. Helen Van Winkle (a.k.a. Baddiewinkle)

Conclusion:

Go digital yesterday. There is no other choice.

WORKBOOK EXERCISE SPACE: